BLACK JACK

THE LIFE STORY OF BOUGHTON'S FOWLER TRACTION ENGINE

ROB BOUGHTON AND
TRAFFORD BOUGHTON

AMBERLEY

First published 2026

Amberley Publishing
The Hill, Stroud,
Gloucestershire, GL5 4EP

www.amberley-books.com

ISBN: 978 1 3981 3026 5 (print)
ISBN: 978 1 3981 3027 2 (ebook)

British Library Cataloguing in Publication Data.
A catalogue record for this book is available from the British Library.

Typeset in 11pt on 14.5pt Celeste.
Typesetting by SJmagic DESIGN SERVICES, India.
Printed in Great Britain.

Appointed GPSR EU Representative: Easy Access System Europe Oü, 16879218
Address: Mustamäe tee 50, 10621, Tallinn, Estonia
Contact Details: gpsr.requests@easproject.com, +358 40 500 3575

Contents

Preface

Black Jack, an 8-hp general-purpose traction engine, was built at the renowned John Fowler and Sons Limited Steam Plough Works in Leeds in 1897. However, his existence began in 1895 at those famous works when a quantity of 8-hp boilers was manufactured, as was the custom to build boilers in batches and store them according to size in the yard until they were required.

Black Jack was given the number 7788, an easy to remember number when in 1896 the building began in earnest of an engine destined to remain in the same family's ownership for over 100 years. For his first fifty years, *Black Jack* threshed corn in and around the counties of Buckinghamshire, Hertfordshire and Middlesex from July (in an early season) through to March or April the following year. For the remainder of the year, he could often be seen hauling road trailers or busily sawing wood.

What tales he could tell and what changes he could relate if he were able! This book aims to detail his history on his behalf. Now, let him tell us his life's story as seen through his oil lamps.

Black Jack's maker's plate.

Introduction

My father, Trafford Boughton, had a photographic memory. He could recall in detail events, places and people from his earliest days. How as a family we would press him to write down some of his recollections; they would have provided a fascinating insight into what was a rapidly changing world.

We never succeeded in getting him to commit pen to paper to recall his life story, but at least he did write these words on the life and times of *Black Jack*, a steam engine that has remained in the ownership of the Boughton family now for 129 years. What a lovely tale he wrote, full of detail of how life was back then when the Boughton family business was getting started. Also, much on the trials and tribulations of traction engine ownership and the men who had the tough job

Mr Trafford Boughton.

Trafford (standing) with his brother and sister accompanied by Frank Honour, *c.* 1922.

of driving these wonderful machines all year round in whatever the weather threw at them.

I have attempted to add a little exposition to some of the writing so that an audience with or without an interest in steam engines can appreciate it fully. I have also reimagined one or two conversations between some of the main characters in the stories to add a little bit of extra colour.

What I have not done, nor would ever want to do, is change the charming way my dear father wrote the tales and how he personified our lovely engine *Black Jack*, who after all is the hero of the story. I hope you enjoy the book.

Rob Boughton

1

My Early Years

It may seem a bit surreal to be addressed by a traction engine, something most people would believe is an inanimate object with no more soul or personality than a washing machine, but as you will know we breathe air, and eat and drink like yourselves so it's not such a leap of faith to take.

I was conceived at the John Fowler and Sons Limited Steam Plough Works in Leeds which was, at that time, a world-famous manufacturer of high-quality steam engines. You could even say that John Fowler was the Rolls-Royce of its day. I would like to think so anyway.

I was destined to become an 8-hp general-purpose steam traction engine. Some might say a 'tool of the trade'. Nothing fancy like a showman's or specialist like a ploughing engine, but important and versatile all the same. Indeed, I would be able to perform multiple tasks if called upon. For example, I could tow trailers of goods and materials, like a modern-day tractor unit. Using my flywheel and a belt I could power many different pieces of machinery like wood saws, water pumps and, perhaps most often, corn threshing machines. You see this was long before the invention of combine harvesters.

I was a popular model and thus to meet that demand John Fowler built engines like me in lots, the equivalent of modern-day batch manufacturing, and so it was that my boiler was made first in 1895 and given the number 7788. However, it ended up laying in the yard for a time; things were bad in the traction engine world, especially for general-purpose engines, despite everything I have just said. You see, the second half of the nineteenth century had been a particularly tough time for Britain's agricultural industry.

But, at last, my turn came to be completed, and slowly but surely, I took shape as all the necessary parts were added until finally I became a complete engine. In early 1897 a kind employee of John Fowler was the first person to light my fire and my life began. As I moved (literally) under my own steam for the very first

Black Jack posing outside the Bell Lane works in Amersham in the mid-1990s.

time, I caught a glimpse of myself in a large horse pond. Gosh, my funnel was large, very large indeed, no one ever told me why. It was almost unique, as there were only a very few like me, but I am glad to say I steamed well during my trial and partial running-in (according to the quality inspectors). Despite the size of my chimney, I could bark loudly if called upon to do so – a positive attribute in any self-respecting engine's repertoire.

The next decision concerning my appearance was what colour I should be painted. Some might have said (not me obviously) that in comparison with engines from Lincoln (John Fowler's main rivals) I was somewhat ugly, but when finished in a nice shade of green or maroon, like most general-purpose engines, I believe I would have come up to muster.

But, when your name is *Black Jack*, what other colour was I destined to be? Of course, I was painted black, like a ploughing engine. But how handsome I looked, even if I do say so myself. My glossy finish was set off with smart red and yellow

Black Jack letting off steam.

lining. I possessed three shining brass bands around my belly, sported bright caps on my flywheel hub and wheels and, to crown it all, a gleaming brass top was resplendently fitted to my now-impressive funnel. It's fair to say that I looked distinctive, even distinguished, as in 1897 polished flywheel hubs complete with front and rear wheel caps on a general-purpose engine were almost unheard of.

So much for my appearance. I had a quite unique specification too. To keep my hungry boiler replenished with water I was fitted with a reciprocating pump and water lift. But for some reason, lost in the annals of time, I was not equipped with a steam injector. My regulator lever was of the 'monkey tail' variety, again, somewhat like a compound ploughing engine, and instead of my driver pushing the lever away to get started, he had to pull my regulator towards him to get me moving. Gently too, because with a full head of steam I have always had a fierce throttle and, in fact, I have never been docile with over 100 lb of steam pressure within my boiler.

The day soon came for my first trip. I was leaving what had been my home all my life, and with a sense of excitement and a little trepidation I was on my way. All the way to the railway siding. There I was loaded onto a waggon and transported to Southampton and then on to the famous Bath and West Agricultural Show. Quite a few of us Fowler family engines went on that train: ploughing engines; road locos; road rollers; and me and one other general-purpose engine with a smaller funnel. The show lasted a week and whilst several farmers showed interest, they would each walk away shaking their heads, and as a result I was unsold.

I knew it. It was my funnel. It had to be because large was not fashionable. I also found out why my Fowler roller and road loco friends had had names already painted on them; they had been sold before we had left Leeds! One was even going to India. But for me, after several days, I was loaded up again and, this time with fewer others, I went on a trip to Reading in Berkshire.

We were now on our way to the Royal Counties Show in Prospect Park. What a display. There were engines like me as far as my oil lamps could see. Engines from every manufacturer in the country it seemed: Aveling & Porters; Claytons; Burrells; Robeys; Ransomes; Rustons; even Garretts from Leiston; and from nearby, Taskers from Andover and Wallis & Steevens of Basingstoke.

Monday, Tuesday and Wednesday went by, and although business was brisk, I was still unsold. Never mind, best wheel forward and all that. Thursday was a nice day, it was hot and the sunshine made my paint gleam as I silently ticked over. This was something I could do better than most and I was determined to show that off. Halfway through the morning's proceedings, I suddenly became aware of some interest in me, more interest than usual; I dared to hope. A party consisting of one young and two much older gentlemen stood talking about me for a long time with

Mr John Boughton with a very young Trafford.

my friend, Mr George Chapman, who was the Fowler salesman. I ticked over as smoothly and quietly as I could but to my dismay the gentlemen eventually walked away, and I was left alone all afternoon. I am sorry to say, I gave up hope for the day.

Towards the early evening, my boiler pressure rose sharply, and my cylinder nearly missed a beat when my oil lamps clocked the three gentlemen returning to the Fowler show stand. What I couldn't know was that the three, who were a Mr John Boughton, a gentleman farmer from Chenies, in Buckinghamshire, his son, Tom Boughton, and Mr John's long-standing engine driver, George Harris, had spent the entire afternoon in lively debate over whether it was worth paying the £400 Mr Chapman wanted in exchange for me.

You see, George Harris was a big fan of Aveling & Porter engines, the ones with the prancing horse on the front (long before Mr Ferrari), whilst young Mr Tom had always wanted a Fowler (such good taste). Mr John did not mind what make of engine it was, so long as it represented value for money, for he was the one paying. He was going to buy an engine for young Mr Tom to help him expand his fledgling business as a twenty-first birthday present.

'Good evening, Mr Chapman. Now, I am sure you won't want to take No. 7788 back with you to Leeds, will you now?' opened Mr John.

'Well not, rightly, Mr Boughton, but the price 'as got to be right, like.'

'Well, we have seen another suitable engine, a Wallis & Steevens, but do prefer your 7788, here.' I held my exhaust. 'We will offer you £350, no more.'

'£375 and he's yours.'

Mr Tom Boughton as a young man.

'Come on, young Tom, we're off to buy the Wallis. 7788 can go back to Yorkshire,' and away they walked. I let off a disappointed hiss of steam and resigned myself to heading back north. But Mr Chapman had other ideas, and after a brief conversation with a colleague, he chased after the Boughton party with his full and final offer in hand.

If I could have blown my own whistle, I would have done, because on their return, a deal was struck, and the gentlemen shook hands for £360. This meant I had an owner and I was part of a new family with a career stretching ahead of me, and, what I didn't know at the time, a very interesting one at that.

I couldn't leave right away, however. I had to wait until the end of the show, but it didn't matter as I spent the remaining days looking forward to my new life. I was so happy I didn't even care about the drunks who leaned on me, or relieved themselves on my wheels, or made rude remarks about my chimney, because at last I had a home, a mission, a future.

This was July 1897, and by now Her Majesty Queen Victoria had been on the throne for sixty years. Her reign had overseen a period of great prosperity and a British Empire which covered a quarter of the globe. Britain was indeed great. To honour the occasion of the queen's diamond jubilee, preparations were undertaken for celebrations and carnivals in every town and village across the land. It truly was a time of real jubilation and thanksgiving in which everybody took part.

Reading was not to be outdone. There was to be a grand procession along with a parade complete with floats of every kind, as well as bands playing and flags flying. Someone was required to lead such an event, and I was overjoyed to learn that I had been chosen for that particular honour.

To make me look suitably regal, I was bedecked with flags in preparation for the great day. Huge amounts of organisation went into the parade, as you can imagine, with much jostling and shouting and bossing around by the show's organisers,

Black Jack leading the parade at the Reading Show in 1897.

but finally everything was in place. It was down to me, a Yorkshire-born general-purpose traction engine with a larger than normal funnel, to get things underway. I was under strict instruction to move at a gentle pace. That was lucky, as I could never go fast anyway.

As I led the way through the streets of Reading town, I witnessed a day of great enjoyment and celebration, with plenty of frivolity and happiness. Once the parade was over and my jubilee bunting was taken down, I said goodbye to my Fowler friends, especially to Mr Chapman, and went to a Harry Lewis' yard near Reading railway station where I rested for a few days. Here I awaited the fitting of a steam injector (which was also part of the sales bargain) and, most importantly, the arrival of my new owners and the beginning of what was to be the most eventful life for such a humble traction engine like me.

2

Reading to Chenies

It was a quiet week in Harry Lewis' yard while I waited to find out how I would get to my new home. I had nothing to do and rested happily in the warm summer weather. When the men came to install the steam injector, which would be a big improvement, I overheard them saying that I was going to be loaded onto a train and taken to Chorleywood station on the Metropolitan Line out of London, which was the nearest stop to my new home.

However, at 9 o'clock in the morning at the end of the week as Harry Lewis lit my fire and got steam up who should enter the yard but my new owner, young Mr Tom Boughton, accompanied by Geoge Harris and another fellow called Jack, having just alighted from the latest London train. They had railed at the railway's charge of £15 to transport me. That was the equivalent of nearly four months' wages for Mr Harris after all, and so they had decided to drive me to my new home instead.

My new friends set about preparing for the journey. From Reading to Chenies was approximately 35 miles and so preparations were extensive. After buying six tube brushes and a bucket for the princely sum of 10*s* and 9*d*, oiling all my joints and gears, filling my cylinder lubricator with a tallow-like substance (I had no mechanical lubrication), stocking up my bunker with coal and my tender with water, and having tied a spare sack of coal to my running board, we set forth. A few toots from my whistle by way of a cheerio to my friends in Reading and I took my first turns towards my future.

The gang assumed their positions. George Harris took charge of my regulator, Mr Tom was at my steering wheel and Jack's station was walking in front to deal with oncoming horse traffic. We travelled cautiously in low gear to begin with for the first mile or so until we were out of Reading, where we paused to allow George to engage my high gear and we picked up a little bit of speed on the road to Twyford.

It was a warm day, and thus thirsty work. George, a chapel man, was de facto in charge of our little band of brothers and would not allow any of us to stop at a pub along the way for refreshments. Jack found this hard to deal with as he enjoyed his ale, and we all went dry until we arrived at Twyford. By then my tender was nearly empty and I desperately needed a drink to recharge my boiler. Presently, the road crossed a stream, and it offered the perfect opportunity for me to slake my thirst.

George brought me to a halt. My neatly coiled water pipe was unhooked from my running board, which runs from just ahead of my offside running wheel forward to my chimney stump, and connected to me at one end and the other was led to the gurgling stream. My lift pump was turned on and a few short moments later, my tender was effortlessly brimming with nice, cool, fresh water.

The operation was now reversed, and Mr Tom, who had been delegated with the task, leapt back up into my cab and with a nod from George we rumbled off again in low gear through the bucolic surroundings of Twyford village en route to Hare Hatch. All was well in the world, the weather was kind, the Berkshire countryside was in full bloom and we were making good progress.

All of a sudden there was a loud, metallic clanging noise accompanied by a jolt and George brought me to a standstill to investigate. Climbing down, he immediately recognised the problem. My hose pipe had unravelled and trailed

The watering hole at Twyford in 2025.

The site of the incident in Twyford in 2025.

along the road until my rear offside wheel ran over the brass strainer and flattened the pipework. My brand-new hose was rendered useless.

As I said, George was a chapel man and would not swear or employ coarse language; he just turned to young Mr Tom, whose job it had been to secure the hose with the simple leather strap, and firmly suggested he swap places with Jack. Considering Mr Tom was technically my owner, it's fair to say he did not take kindly to this change of responsibilities.

Whilst the journey continued, the day got hotter, the sun beat down and progress slowed. At the next pub, spirits rose as George brought me to a stop. Mouths were virtually watering, but instead of a couple of pints of cool, frothing and refreshing ale, George came out of the establishment with a jug of water and a newly purchased bucket. Spirits took a dive amongst my crew, not only because of the lack of beer, but because of the realisation that with no hose pipe they would have to replenish my water tank from here to home by hand. There were many ponds and streams along the way and whilst Mr Tom and Jack tipped buckets of water into my tender, George busied himself oiling my bearings and tending to my cylinder lubrication. The tension increased hour by hour.

It was Friday 14 July, and it was late in the day by the time the sun began to sink below the horizon. We pressed on, however, having only paused to light my paraffin lamps, white to the front and red to the rear, and, eventually, in the gathering gloom a welcome inn appeared ahead, near Knowl Hill, and Jack steered me into its yard and there we stayed the night, or what was left of it.

Before my friends could retire to bed, I had to be banked up for the night. George made up my fire with slack coal, closed my ash pan lid and clambered up onto my running board to place a damper on the top of my chimney. Finally, using the new injector, he filled my boiler with water, patted me on the wheel and left me to settle down in the warm summer night. Despite the travails of the day, my spirits were high and by the light of the full moon I rested contently. But not for long.

At around 4.15 a.m., George sent Mr Tom out to take the damper off and open my ash pan lid to revive my snoozing fire. Half an hour later I had a full head of steam, and at 5 o'clock, just as the stars began to be exchanged for the first rays of sun across the morning sky, we were underway again.

Our route took us through the town of Maidenhead, across old Father Thames then up Taplow Hill past a large, thatched house (more of that later). We continued northwards towards the Buckinghamshire town of Beaconsfield. As we approached Cliveden House, we pulled up at the Feathers public house. This pub, which is still there today, was known locally as the Prince of Wales' Feathers, because our then future king would often pop in for a pint on his way to and from Windsor. I was hoping he was there that morning, but not only did George disappoint me by reporting no royal presence but he also upset Jack and Mr Tom by, once again, only bringing out a jug of water by way of refreshment.

To add insult to injury to Mr Tom and Jack, I needed a water refill and so another half hour of lugging pails of water to my tender followed whilst, once again,

The Feathers public house.

George managed to just finish attending to my bearings and lubricator as the last bucket was being poured into my tank. I could at least take comfort from George's diligence!

I had been steaming well all the way and would have made better progress if it wasn't for the labourious process of topping up my water tank. Consequently, George concluded that unless our pace could be increased, he would not be able to attend chapel on Sunday and so stops were kept to a minimum. We were all hungry, though, and something needed to be done about that. George bought me a hundredweight of coal in Beaconsfield and as we trundled through Seer Green, he procured some bread and cheese for Mr Tom, Jack and himself.

By the middle of the afternoon, having passed through the hamlet of Jordans, where we saw the Quaker meeting house, and onwards in front of the famous poet John Milton's cottage, where he sat down to write *Paradise Lost*, we stopped once more to fill up my tank from the pond in the village of Chalfont St Giles.

As George assiduously refilled his oil can once again, I watched young Mr Tom heaving bucket after sloshing bucket into my water tank. The look on his face said everything. How he wished he had taken more care securing my hose pipe outside

The village pond in Chalfont St Giles.

Chenies Manor in 2025.

Twyford. He must have been telling himself that if he had, by now he would be raising a tankard with unblistered hands at the Bedford Arms in Chenies, far away from the censorious eye of George.

Happily, however, from Chalfont St Giles we were on the home straight. Having crossed the London Road and climbed out of the village, we turned right down Roughwood Lane, along Lodge Lane past Church Grove to turn right for Chenies. By early evening my tired oil lamps caught sight of the many-chimneyed Tudor pile that was Chenies Manor. Mr Tom's father, Mr John Boughton, lived in the manor house which formed part of the vast estate of the Dukes of Bedford. It certainly was a grand house for a farmer to live in, but it came with the tenancy.

News of my pending arrival had obviously travelled before us because as we approached Poundfield Gate, which marked the entrance to the farm, a large crowd of villagers had gathered to welcome us. Back then, to enter the 10-ft-wide Poundfield Gate required a much sharper left-hand turn than today, because they were yet to realign the main road to make it easier. It was a tricky turn with any vehicle, but when the steersman is relatively inexperienced and I was equipped with a limited steering lock, the upcoming manoeuvre was going to be a challenge.

The site of Poundfield Gate in 2025.

The pressure was on, particularly with the boisterous crowd ready with a quick judgement.

To counter my shallow turning ability, Jack should have first swung out to the right before beginning the turn proper to the left. It was going to be close, but as we continued our turn we were doing nicely. Suddenly, just at the crucial moment, a waggish onlooker bellowed, 'Whoa! Watch out, you'll hit the gate!'

Now George, who was used to an 1871 vintage Aveling engine, docile in character and with a regulator that pushed to open and pulled to shut, must have felt the pressure of the moment too, for in response to the warning, he pulled sharply back on my throttle. Instead of stopping, as George expected, I had no choice but to respond in what was to become my characteristic way. Full steam was released into my cylinder, and with such an impulse, my front wheels rose up off the road and crashed down on the gate and its accompanying post with a resounding, timber-shattering smash.

Well, the assembled crowd laughed and jeered, and many an indistinguishable ribald comment could be heard. I stood there deeply embarrassed, my front wheels resting on the splintered timbers which once formed the handsome gate, with my new paintwork painfully scratched. I wasn't the only one who felt the heat, though, because amidst the confusion George had collected his coat and dinner basket and was seen striding back towards Chalfont St Giles and home.

Having heard the commotion, Mr John Boughton mounted his horse and rode up to discover his new purchase poised over his shattered gate and one of his employees stomping home in a funk. Who was going to help me complete my journey now? George had already covered some ground so Mr John spurred his horse and galloped after him before he could get much further.

Jack, Mr Tom and I sat there steaming quietly as a prolonged discussion ensued between George and his boss, whilst the crowd, sensing that they had probably witnessed the highlight of the day, started to drift away.

Eventually George returned and drove me into the yard, marking an anticlimactic conclusion to what had been an eventful journey. I know Mr John had not expected to replace my hose so soon or repair my paintwork or cover the extra expense of the additional bucket but as I sat there gently cooling down after what had been a hot and often bothersome couple of days, I had to listen to George's demanding negotiations with Mr John.

'I said Fowlers were no good. I've never liked 'em, and, in course, everyone knows that Avelings are better, all 'round.' I lowered my lamps as he decried my friends in Leeds. Mr John just stood and listened with a look of tired resignation. Despite George's singular character traits, he was a sober and reliable employee who was hard working and dependable.

Black Jack's steering stops cut away.

'You won't get me droivin it again until it can turn tighter, and the regulator works t'other way round. Which, that's my final word on the matter, Good Night to you ... Sir.'

I wasn't an 'it'. I was *Black Jack*.

So, in addition to the parts that needed replacing, I was to be subjected to the dubious surgical skills of the local blacksmith. To this day I have never been very proud of the new regulator bracket the smithy fashioned or, for that matter, the way in which my steering stops were cut away to allow for tighter turns.

Sadly, me, a brand-new general-purpose traction engine, a product of the great Steam Works in Leeds, ended up being mutilated to please an obstinate old man. As they say, you can't teach an old dog new tricks.

3

Settling In

It was quite easy to settle into my new home because I had nothing much to do until harvest. Mr Tom and his men, however, were very busy. Part of Mr Tom's business was importing and selling corn binders to customers in the Home Counties. The binders arrived in boxes from Chicago, in the USA, and required assembling before being despatched to their various destinations. They sold well.

However, as the summer rolled on, thoughts turned to harvest time and the important role I was going to play. My job was to go to farms and thresh corn. To do

Black Jack connected up to his threshing machine.

this, I had to be paired up with a threshing machine, which I would tow behind me along with a living van for my crew to the farm that hired us. Once there, I would be rigged up. This involved placing a large canvas belt around my fly wheel and then looping this around the threshing machine's drive pulley. The harvested crop would be fed from the ricks at one end, and by some dark mechanical magic in the middle, out came grains of corn at the other. All this needed motive power, so I would sit there all day, in neutral, powering the operation.

The threshing machine I was to partner was old; it was a single crank shaker made by Clayton and Shuttleworth at Lincoln in about 1870. Mr John Boughton had had it repaired and repainted in preparation and although it was slow, it could turn out a good sample of corn. My old 'friend' George Harris had worked the machine from new and was well acquainted with its shortcomings, which made things easier, and we set off for our first job close to the nearby town of Chesham. It turned out that the problems we encountered on our trip from Reading were insignificant compared with that journey.

You wouldn't believe the problems a traction engine like me were supposed to have caused in my young days. From the beginning of time until the advent of steam engines, the animal kingdom had reigned supreme and in the late 1890s, our four-legged friends still claimed they had not received sufficient notice to adapt their ways to the likes of me and my brethren.

When I came rumbling down a hill or chuffing up one, cows and sheep would run away in fright to the farthest point of their field. Dogs barked and jumped up at gates and, most worryingly, horses, with whom I shared the road, would tend to shy or bolt in uncontrollable terror. To try and counter this problem, up until 1895, it was a legal obligation to have a man with a red flag precede any self-propelled vehicle to provide early warning of the impending peril.

Black Jack threshing. A spare cutting blade is leaning against his tender.

In 1897, although the man and flag were no longer required, it remained customary to have someone lead horses past while the engine stood still and patiently waited. During my journey from Reading, we had experienced several such horses which had shied, and even bolted, but thankfully, no harm had come to anyone. We had also met with a few 'horseless carriages' along the way, and horses were, if anything, more frightened of them as they travelled faster and made a horrible noise when they approached. The 'pop, pop, pop' of a single-cylinder internal combustion engine, not to mention the bitter waft of semi-burnt petrol in their nostrils, was intolerable to anything on four legs and the result of such a meeting was frequently nothing short of a stampede.

First then we went to thresh wheat at Loudham's Farm, near Chalfont, and our next job was between Chesham and Berkhamsted. We proceeded steadily enough until we were descending New Road into Chesham. At the steepest part, we met a pony and trap; the horse was young, the couple middle-aged. The gentleman driver panicked, the steed reared and backed the rear wheels into a ditch. The shafts of the trap snapped, and the occupants were lobbed into the hedge and although, thankfully, the passengers were more humiliated than hurt, they insisted on calling the police. In those days it took a long time to get help, and it was an hour or so before the constable came peddling up the hill. As he recovered his composure, he listened carefully to the lady's account of what had happened and consequently we were threatened with prosecution.

'But we did nothing wrong, Sorr,' exclaimed George. 'That there hoss just shied and drove their gig into the ditch.' I exhausted some steam in agreement. Despite

Amersham Road leading down to Chesham, where *Black Jack* encountered the pony and trap.

our protestations, it was a long time before we were underway again. Fortunately, we were insured against such happenings and went to court to fight our case, but the process dragged on and on. Mr Tom managed to avoid paying damages but, due to a technicality whereby the insurance company escaped liability, we were saddled with the court costs that consumed my entire first year's profits.

I couldn't have been the only one to have such encounters, because it became more and more difficult to find anyone prepared to insure a traction engine as the claims against the owners were terrific. Roads had only been designed for horse-drawn vehicles, most bridges were inadequate and many an unfortunate engine crashed through into the river or canal below and, in the early days, plenty of firms went into liquidation as a result.

Naturally, because they felt threatened, the horse-drawn fraternity and the railways had waged a fierce war against all forms of road locomotion, and the battle was still raging when the first 'horseless carriages' appeared on the scene. The legal battle to get rid of the man with the red flag had seethed both long and loud in and out of both Houses of Parliament and this debate continued during the first five years of my existence.

By 1899, Mr Tom's business had grown and was now a profitable undertaking. However, it was still a very seasonal affair, with binder assembly keeping everyone at full pitch in the late spring and early summer. But what were Mr Tom's employees to do in the autumn and winter? The answer to this prickly question was threshing; after all, that was why I was purchased in the first place. We had generated plenty of business, but the problem was accessing the resources to undertake it. Therefore, Mr Tom wrote to my old friend George Chapman, and I was delighted to hear that a brother engine was soon on order from Leeds.

However, the newspapers were full of reports about some sort of trouble halfway across the world in South Africa and it was decided to send the British Army there

A bridge that wasn't designed to take traction engines.

to deal with the problem. We didn't worry too much about it as they said it would all be over in a few weeks, but to cut a long and very sad story short, the war went on and on. You may well ask how all this conflict so far away could affect life in Chenies, deep in the Chiltern Hills. Well, the engine Mr Tom had ordered from Fowler's became one of many commandeered by the British government to be dispatched to the South African war. I mean, what good would a slow old engine like me be in the dry and mountainous regions where the war was fought? How long would his hose need to be to reach the nearest waterhole? Sadly, like many brave men and engines, it never returned home, and I was not to be joined by my Yorkshire sibling. The whole affair was a big disappointment to the firm because we had the business, we had the men, just not enough equipment. Alternative solutions needed to be found.

Our neighbour in Chenies, Lord Chesham, had an old Fowler, No. 3190, which had been used partly for farm work but mainly to haul coal from the LNWR railway station at Boxmoor, about 6 miles distant, to feed the hungry fireplaces on his Latimer estate. When not busy doing those chores, he also lent a wheel at sawing wood and even generating electricity for Latimer House when the River Chess was low or the water turbine needed an overhaul. However, by the end of the nineteenth century, the Metropolitan Railway had reached as far as Chesham and coal could now be brought to within a mile of Latimer and so 3190 was no longer needed. Lord Chesham put the engine up for sale and Mr Tom bought him, and his name was *Pincher*. He was a noisy little 6-hp engine, with a small straight funnel and a sloping back to his tender, a characteristic of my older siblings. So, now there were two of us, we were a gang. *Pincher* took over my old Clayton single crank shaker machine and Mr Tom purchased a nearly new Clayton for me from Steventon in Berkshire. I was very proud of my new partner; it was fitted with double crank shakers and a back blower and, in short, it was much more advanced, and we were destined to be partners for nearly fifty years.

No. 3190, *Pincher*.

Black Jack at Chalfont Road station with the dung carts.

Eventually, the war in South Africa ended, and the men came back with all sorts of tales to tell. Things in the Chiltern Hills carried on as usual, with me spending most of the year threshing corn. The season would normally begin in the Rickmansworth valley in August when we threshed wheat straight from the field, but in exceptional years, when the harvest was early, we could start in July.

As summer turned to autumn, I would watch the leaves turn golden, and the blackberries ripen as we moved from the open fields to work amongst the barns and ricks. All through the winter, farmyards would echo to the sound of threshing while the sweet smell of steam and oil drifted through these timeless buildings. We would soldier on through the bitter months of January and February and usually finish in March when the brisk winds would whip the smoke from my funnel, but exceptionally we could continue all the way until May.

In the intervening days until the next season of threshing commenced, I was employed in the haulage of manure from the Metropolitan Line's Chalfont Road station to Mr John's farms and other places in the district to fertilise the fields. There were two waggons to pull, and I had to complete two journeys a day. The dung came straight from the streets of London and due to the almost limitless supply, the railway company constructed extra-long sidings at the station to accommodate the full-length trains. Needless to say, it was a smelly job and over the years I must have hauled hundreds, perhaps thousands, of tons of the stinky stuff. But, as they say, where there's muck...

4

Changing Times

The business had expanded rapidly up to 1902, but my owner Mr Tom, was deeply frustrated. It was the same old problem. Plenty of corn to thresh but not enough engines and sets to meet the demand. John Fowler and Son had had to supply their entire production to the army, leaving nothing for the home market whatsoever. Mr Tom turned to the second-hand market for answers as the purchase of old *Pincher* had been successful. Another venerable Fowler was acquired from the firm Morris of Aylesbury, together with an aged Aveling, built in 1874. The Fowler was

Granny hidden amongst the hayricks, threshing. Mr Tom has his back to the camera.

named *Central* and numbered 3184. The old Aveling, No. 1262, was aptly called *Granny*, and she was a convertible road roller and thus with this purchase Mr Tom opened up another line of work.

The Boughton gang was growing and not only was the range of what we could do expanding but so was the business's reach. In short, we were no longer confined to the Chiltern Hills. Mr Tom had been a long-time friend of T. C. Jones of Shepherd's Bush and I, *Black Jack*, a general-purpose traction engine from Leeds, was given the task of hauling the first load of scrap iron into Joe Latter's pig farm in Shepherd's Bush, which T. C. Jones had acquired for his new depot. Later, this site was to become the West London headquarters of The 600 Group, the engineering conglomerate.

In 1903, His Grace the Duke of Bedford visited Chenies. By this time, the yard at the back of Chenies Manor was a hive of activity. Casting his lofty eye around he couldn't help but observe a collection of steam engines and witness the mass assembling of binders. He was infuriated by what he saw and decreed, 'Under no circumstances, young Boughton, will I have any industry, with its dark and satanic mills, in the village of *my* ancestors.'

This pronouncement came as a big blow to my young master, but it was not surprising. Up and down the country the landed gentry were fighting and, in most

A busy scene at Bell Lane in the 1930s.

cases, winning the battle to prevent progress on their estates. Not too far away, the Earl of Essex, amongst others, had prevented the London & North Western Railway from taking their route through the centre of Tring. The line was diverted a fair distance away, and thus, forever prevented Tring benefitting from fast and efficient transport links up and down the country.

Consequently, Mr Tom had to find a new home for his business. Until then the firm had enjoyed a rent-free base, which had been very helpful in the early years. Luckily, not all aristocrats were of the same mind. Mr Tom journeyed the short distance to Latimer to wait on Lord Chesham to inquire if he had any spare land suitable for a growing business. Consequently, we moved a couple of miles west to Bell Lane in Amersham Common, to a site alongside the Joint Metropolitan & Great Central Railway, between the stations of Chalfont Road and Amersham.

Coincidental with the move, Mr Tom purchased from the famous engineer Jesse Ellis a quantity of road rollers which had once helped to construct the Thames Embankment, part of the great London sewer project, designed by another famous engineer, Sir Joseph Bazalgette. Incidentally, Jesse Ellis started his career working for Aveling & Porter, in Kent, and so it was apt that all the rollers purchased were Avelings, Nos 1462, 2725, 3401 and 4033. Interestingly, No. 1462 had originally been fitted with conical wheels.

An old Aveling & Porter roller.

In addition to the Ellis rollers, Mr Tom also bought two high-wheeled traction engines from Croydon, one named *Ethel,* who was complete, and the other actually called *Croydon,* who was in pieces. The whole deal was brokered by my owner's famous friend, Mr T. C. Jones, who, by the by, ran a compound Aveling No. 4755 to do his heavy haulage, of which more later.

While I continued my threshing career, *Ethel,* who was a strapping lass, did the heavy haulage. *Croydon* was delighted to be rebuilt, and he joined our threshing gang. We were now a sizeable band and finally Mr Tom had sufficient plant and equipment to satisfy the demands of the local farming community.

All across the Chilterns' farmland and beyond the pleasant aromas of the animal kingdom and the sweet scent of coal smoke mixed with warm cylinder oil drifted through the farmyard buildings, wafted over the fields and floated amongst the beautiful woodlands that adorned the area. This fine perfume, as I liked to think of it, was a nostalgic product of the age of steam and had always been closely associated with transport. I both radiated heat and emitted a mixture of scents absent from any other sphere, fragrant to many, abhorrent to but a few. However, winds of change were in the air that not only brought sad tidings via discarded newspapers but also novel and more pungent smells from beyond our horizons.

The news that Queen Victoria had died was taking a lot of getting used to. She had reigned for over sixty-three years. Could there ever to be another reign like that? After such a long wait, her eldest son, Bertie, was now King Edward VII, and the Edwardian era was getting established, heralding much change.

The new and rather repellent smell that now permeated the scene was the harsh repugnant odour of burnt hydrocarbons discarded by the early 'horseless carriages'. Like many an imposter, this pong was a bully, and it aggressively displaced the

Croydon hard at work.

Black Jack, busy earning his keep in the winter's snow.

sweeter, gentler smell of steam engines. Across the globe more was changing than just the atmosphere and the world would soon never be the same again. The leisurely pace of life, when things moved no faster than a horse, or traction engine, was rapidly becoming a thing of the past and speed was taking over.

Mr Tom, however, was always one to adapt to the times and embrace new ideas and opportunities, but it was with mixed feelings that one morning I watched him drive into the yard, at the wheel of a motor car, an Argyll that had been made in Scotland. Not long afterwards he purchased a Fiat which he converted into a pick-up truck. This could have been, quite possibly, the origin of the species. He used it to deliver oil and other necessities to his threshing tackle and steamrollers that were spread around the Chilterns, near and far.

Of course, I belonged to a more languid age. It took me an age to get up steam, I needed constant attention from an oil can and, at best, I could do 3 miles an hour. In addition, I had to have my boiler washed out every 100 hours, which would take a few days, and my boiler tubes leaked on occasion (my driver's fault invariably), which again required timely and time-consuming attention.

But these newfangled cars, as the 'horseless carriages' came to be known as, had to be pushed, towed and coaxed up the hills on a regular basis. Many a time would I be overtaken, in a cloud of acrid fumes by an impatient driver, only to find him bending over the engine a mile or so up the road. I couldn't resist a toot as we rumbled past. In short, I was dependable and reliable and never gave up.

As the rhythm of the changing seasons continued in our small, but lovely corner of the world, it didn't seem long before we received the news that Edward VII had died, and his son crowned King George V. It was concerning to note that amid the coronation celebrations fears about the future tempered people's enjoyment. Storm clouds were gathering over the horizon; was the world changing too fast?

A fine aerial view of our hero.

Right: *Black Jack* recovering another 'horseless carriage'.

Below: It was hard work, especially in winter.

We kept busy as ever, fulfilling the incoming enquiries, but it wasn't easy as our drivers seemed to be drinking more and more. I began life with the teetotal, chapel man George Harris before Sam Larkin took over the wheel until, in 1907, my dear friend George Ruff, who was a steady and sensible man, became my driver. He drove me during the threshing season for thirty-one years until my partial retirement in 1939. Some of my companions were less fortunate. Traction engines were robust and resilient, and we caused very few accidents by mechanical failure or explosion. Instead, I am afraid to say, nearly every mishap was a direct result of the demon drink.

Poor old *Central* had a terrible accident, for example, when he ran away down White Hill in Chesham and ended up on his side with his threshing machine almost on top of him and pieces of his chaff cutter scattered across the road. *Central* had no differential gears and was known as a 'pin engine' because heavy steel pins engaged the main wheels with the drive axle, but on this occasion his driver had, for manoeuvrability, been travelling along the level with only one pin engaged. *Central* was en route from Ley Hill to Chesham and, having recently paused at the Hen & Chickens public house, his driver was in no state (one assumes) to recall the fact that if you only drive one wheel, you only restrain one wheel. What's more, very few engines had brakes which acted directly on the road wheels. *Central* certainly did not.

As they headed down the menacingly steep hill into Chesham, *Central*'s one pinned wheel skidded (iron shod wheels and macadam did not mix well together, as you can imagine) and the whole circus gathered pace. With his crankshaft, gearing and one wheel at a standstill, it became impossible for his befuddled driver to steer at the gathering speed and over went poor *Central* and a whole year's profit with him. Mercifully, his crew was thrown safely clear.

Around that time, T. C. Jones unexpectedly delivered that aforementioned compound road engine, Aveling No. 4755, to our yard at Amersham. She was called

The Hen & Chickens public house in 2025.

Central after his accident.

White Hill in Chesham in 2025.

Moonlight. There was no accompanying letter or phone call, the engine and two trailers just turned up, out of the blue. The driver and mate handed them over: 'T.C.'s had enough of them, there traction engines, you see Mr Tom,' they explained. 'He'll be over one day soon to do the deal with you, Sorr, I'll make no doubt. Now where's the nearest ale house?'

Later, I learned from my driver, George, that *Moonlight* had collided with the Dover mail motor lorry with disastrous results, and T. C. had had enough. So, *Moonlight* joined our team. We made her welcome and because she was a stout lady, she was soon kept very busy hauling timber from the surrounding beech woods to the various sawmills in Chesham and High Wycombe, with Sid Bateman as her driver.

Moonlight had been designed to carry 180 lb per square inch of steam pressure in her boiler, but under inspection it was discovered that she was running at 200. Sid Bateman's brother-in-law explained how twenty minutes could be saved if Sid did not have to change down gear on Amersham Hill or Deadsman's Dene on the 9-mile journey back to our yard with her empty trailers. These hills were some of the most notorious hazards in the locale and made us engines nervous. In order not to have to change gear required extra steam in *Moonlight's* boiler, hence the screwing down of her safety valve. She must have felt awfully bloated and fit to burst.

I suppose you would describe *Moonlight* as an unlucky engine. She suffered many calamities. If there was a road subsidence, she'd get stuck in it. If the hill was steep, you could bet your chimney she'd slip on it, especially if the road surface was constructed with granite sets such as at Bushey Hill, Watford, or Scots Hill, Rickmansworth.

It was late one Saturday afternoon that the news reached Amersham that poor *Moonlight* had three trailers of boxwood that were destined for the woodturners of

No. 4755, *Moonlight*.

Chesham turn turtle. At first, we couldn't believe it because the accident happened at Scots Hill and Mr Tom's drivers were forbidden to use Scots Hill. The standing order was to use the low road from Watford to Rickmansworth, but that was nearly 3 miles further than the more direct route over the hill with its treacherous downwards slope. But it was a Saturday and Will Hearn, who was driving *Moonlight*, believed he could possibly save sixty minutes by taking the short cut; and an extra hour's drinking in the pub was worth the risk. Unfortunately for Will and his men, this idea backfired as they had to spend the evening and the whole of Sunday straightening the trailer's drawbar, reloading the timber and generally clearing up the mess.

Moonlight was always in some sort of trouble. Not long after the Scots Hill accident, she ventured too near the roadside to pick up water in Harefield and slid into the ditch and there she remained until a gang of men travelled from Amersham with jacks and other tackle to extract her. But despite her mishaps, *Moonlight* was always busy hauling heavy loads such as Lancashire boilers and timber from the Chiltern woodlands.

Perhaps the most devilish problem that all steel-wheeled traction engines faced were tramlines. Mr Tom and his men spent ages working out complicated

Moonlight's accident on Scots Hill, Rickmansworth.

Scots Hill in 2025.

routes to avoid them, but it simply wasn't possible to dodge them altogether, and if I, or one of my friends, met a set on a slight incline, and a rear tread was on the steel rail, the wheel would spin, introducing potential disaster. Old hessian sacks were placed under the wheels in such circumstances to get us out of trouble.

5

The End of an Era

During the summer of 1914, and although I continued to thresh corn as usual, across the English Channel, Germany invaded Belgium and soon Britain was at war. For the first few weeks, little changed on the farms, after all the wise men in charge said the war would be over by Christmas. Despite that prediction the army was on a full recruitment drive and many young men from the farms and fields volunteered to join their local regiment.

However, as autumn progressed, the tempo on the farms increased and more and more land was put to the plough. There would be plenty of corn to thresh next season. As soon as the threshing had finished in the spring of 1915, I was dispatched to the Royal Flying Corp's Halton Camp, near Wendover, with three of my engine companions to haul timber and aggregate. These materials were needed to build an aerodrome; a new era had truly arrived.

The road through Wendover and on to Halton was not suitable for such heavy loads and soon it became little more than a filthy white track in the chalk with ruts 2-ft deep. To keep traffic moving, the decision was taken to bring in hundreds of tons of stone to fill the ruts. This task had to be done while keeping the road open to traffic and, as you can imagine, confusion reigned.

It became impossible to make the short journey on wet days, the chalk subsoil and the new stone being simply churned into a slimy mess, but somehow the work carried on. We found it laborious and exhausting work and more than once I got stuck with my load and had to be winched out. Luckily, while all this was going on, a railway line was quickly being laid from Wendover station to Halton Camp, so after a few months I was able to return to my threshing.

It was a busy threshing season, with all the extra fields being planted to wheat, but it was work I enjoyed. It reminded me of the days before the war when somehow, despite the challenges, life felt simpler. However, once the threshing season was over, my fellow engine friends and I were sent off again, this time to

Above: A Clayton and Shuttleworth threshing.

Left: A Fowler single threshing.

Salisbury Plain, a long way from Amersham. We had no time to be homesick, as we were promptly set to work hauling gravel from Fovent, a town in south-west Wiltshire, to the new army camps that were springing up all over the Plain.

We were there for four months and were billeted with dozens of other engines. Mr Tom was very kind, he visited us about once a month, travelling to Salisbury by train and cycling out from the station to wherever we happened to be working. It was comforting to see our owner and helped keep us strong during those dark times. Thankfully, we were sent home for the next threshing season but still the wretched war continued. So, in 1917 off we went to Wiltshire once more to continue the work we had started the year before. We encountered a motley collection of engines there: Burrells; Fowlers; Avelings; Taskers from nearby Andover; Wallis & Steevens; engines from Wantage Engineering; Brown & May from Devizes as well as Lincoln (most of which bore Fletcher hallmarks); Ransomes from Ipswich; and Garretts from Leiston. The war was hoovering up every single resource; every available form of transport, efficient and inefficient, was pressed into service. Their country needed them.

The work was hard and the hours long, but the advantage was that time passed quickly and soon the 1917 threshing season was upon us and we were recalled to Buckinghamshire. Once again, my friends and I had to face the arduous journey back to Amersham. However, it was now a familiar trail, and we knew where to find all the watering places. Getting access to water was always the biggest problem on any trip.

My friends and I were eager to get underway. We headed out of Salisbury, the road taking us past the Pheasant at Winterslow Hut; luckily, that day, there were no marauding lions to attack us. Having taken our fill of water there, we continued up the long drag and then turned left towards Andover via Middle Wallop, past the Anna Valley turning where Taskers were situated. Then we continued via Whitchurch and Laverstock to Basingstoke, past the Wallis & Steevens works and towards Sherfield-on-Loddon. From there we headed through the village of Three Mile Cross (where the author Mary Russell Mitford lived and who, in a connection with home, was related to the Dukes of Bedford) and then on through Reading.

From there we began to retrace the journey I undertook almost exactly twenty years before. This time there were three of us in convoy and we drove at a much greater pace, but with more stops because each driver took it in turns to have a drink at every open pub we passed. We went through Twyford, and then on towards Hare Hatch where I'd ran over my hose pipe on the first-time round. Poor Mr Tom took a long while to get over that calamitous event.

However, twenty years later, there was to be a much more serious episode and one that could have bankrupted our firm. *Croydon*, the old Marshall, and I approached Taplow Hill on Saturday afternoon. Our drivers, anxious to reach home that night, drove us up the hill in top gear, rounding the bend to the left at the steepest part of the hill. We had to work hard up that incline in high gear and both *Croydon* and I were puffing heavily. Just before the gates to Cliveden there stood a thatched house; it is still there but today it has a tiled roof. Sparks, it was alleged, from one or all of us, set the house on fire. We were all oblivious to this at the time, but it turned out to be a total disaster.

The entrance to Clivedon House in 2025.

Our firm was presented with a very large bill for the damage. Mr Tom passed the claim on to his insurance company, but to his utter dismay they declined to cover the costs on the grounds we had not had suitable spark arrestors fitted to the top of our funnels. Mr Tom faced an action that could have finished his business. What was he to do? Thankfully, help was at hand. The news of his predicament had spread, and amazingly, his farmer friends, his insurance agent and a well-known local auctioneer all banded together to save the day. This highly influential group put the case to the insurance company that they should settle the claim because if it did not, the group would take their insurance business elsewhere. The company reflected on this, saw sense, paid the claim and, to our great relief, we were saved.

The war continued, and the Boughton firm grew steadily. We now had twelve sets of threshing tackle, eight road rollers as well as a pair of old Fowler ploughing engines and one extra 8-hp ploughing engine for good measure. Always innovative and adaptable, Mr Tom set the 8-hp ploughing engine to work hauling timber. It would stand outside the woodlands where the ground was more solid. The engine's heavy rope was paid out by a horse and attached to the tree. Then using its powerful winch, the timber would be dragged out to a clearing. Then our sturdy, old friend *Moonlight* loaded and hauled the logs to a sawmill at Hemel Hempstead to be transformed into building materials.

A compound Fowler threshing with Alf Chilton in charge.

Black Jack working hard in winter.

Left: Another Fowler single busily threshing.

Below: Mr Tom with a Fowler ploughing engine, originally destined for Russia.

Finally, the terrible war came to an end and things started to return to how they had been, but we soon realised life was never going to be the same again, with so many young men and, not to forget, engines like me lost in the defence of our freedom. Some equipment did return, however, and just to the west of Slough, about 25 miles from our yard, over 500 acres were set aside as a dump for ex-War Office vehicles and stores. It was an enormous site containing hundreds of lorries, steam waggons and every conceivable article of surplus war stock you could imagine. My dear boss Mr Tom realised straight away the business potential in

Moonlight shifting a heavy load in Chesham.

Moonlight hard at work.

such an 'Aladdin's Cave', and he paid many a visit to Slough to purchase all sorts of vehicles, equipment, spanners, hammers, picks and shovels, both for his own use and for sale to local farmers. He did quite a trade in surplus war equipment for some while and on many occasions did us engines venture westwards to collect items.

It was about this time that the sawmill in Hemel Hempstead burnt down; it happened in the early hours one Monday morning and, guess what, poor *Moonlight* was involved. Her third man, one Sammy Tomlin, slept rough with the engine and it was his job to raise steam by 6 a.m., when the driver and mate would turn up for the week's work. As they arrived, they could see plumes of smoke and jetting flames, the sawmill was ablaze! *Moonlight* was in a meadow 50 yds away, and for once it was nothing to do with her. However, the mill's owner placed the blame fairly and squarely on poor Sammy Tomlin, alleging he must have gone into the mill in the early hours to get lighting wood for the engine and caused the fire to start.

The case went to court. As a witness for the prosecution, the mill's owner was asked why he believed that was the cause of the blaze. 'Well, you see, your Honour, on Sunday I went for an evening stroll, and I saw all this quality wood in his engine's tender. I said to myself, I said, that wood's too good to burn, so while Tomlin was down the pub, I removes it from the engine back to the mill. So, you see, he must have gone down early that morning to get the wood back and tapped his pipe out or something like that.'

'Thank you Mr Millowner, no further questions.' When it was Sammy's turn to defend himself, the prosecuting counsel asked, 'Is this not the case Mr Tomlin, that you set fire to the mill, when you went to fetch that wood?'

'I did not,' exclaimed Sammy emphatically. 'Which Mister the sawmill proprietor does not know was that I had kept the lighting wood in the smoke box all night, to keep it dry, like. Which, *Moonlight* has no awning, you see!'

Somehow, dear old *Moonlight* always seemed to be involved, or witness to some form of trouble or other, and bless her, it was rarely ever her fault. At that time, Bungie Harris was her regular driver. George Harris, my original driver, was his uncle, and Bungie was paired up with several different men as first mate. In 1920, Jack Pearce, who was the younger brother of Lew the workshop foreman at Amersham, returned from the army and took over the job as *Moonlight's* first mate. Sammy Tomlin was still the third man.

Moonlight and her gang were entrusted with the job of hauling timber from Welwyn to the rebuilt Hemel Hempstead sawmill. The timetable went something like this. *Moonlight* and her team would depart Hemel Hempstead on Monday mornings and travel to Welwyn, where they loaded her two trailers with oak trees, which had been extracted from a very large woodland by the 8-hp Fowler

Moonlight putting her strength to good use.

ploughing engine. Each trailer could carry about 250 cubic feet of timber. They would stay overnight in Welwyn and on Tuesday, head off to Hemel Hempstead to unload under the mill crane, then grab a few hours' sleep before returning to Welwyn at first light, load up the trailers again and then nip down to the local pub for a couple of hours of relaxation.

Jack had been a prisoner of war but despite that experience he was a jovial fellow and had developed a bit of a line in amateur entertainment. He had a true voice and could play the piano and was a favourite at the public house in Welwyn, where the team stayed on the Monday and Wednesday nights. Now, the landlady of this establishment was always pleased to see Jack; with him at the piano she was assured a full house, and she may have taken a bit of shine to him too. Unfortunately, however, poor Jack was subject to periodical bouts of illness, the unavoidable consequence of years of deprivation in German prisoner-of-war camps and occasionally he was too ill to come to work. You can imagine the landlady's disappointment when one week Bungie and Sam walked into her pub. 'Where's young Jack then? Is he still out the back?' she enquired of Bungie, who had developed quite the reputation as an inveterate leg-puller.

It wasn't just *Moonlight* who got into trouble.

Bungie's face fell, he scrunched his cap in his hands and in a voice burdened with emotion exclaimed, 'Oh, a terrible thing has happened, Madam, he has only gone and been run over by an engine and surgeon says there's no hope for him.'

Well, the poor woman almost swooned and became hysterical. Bungie and Sam did their best to console her, but no amount of effort, it seemed, could soften such a blow. Imagine the scene the following Monday when the grieving landlady was woken from her early evening nap by a familiar tune on the piano. On entering the bar, she promptly fainted at the sight and sound of 'her' Jack in full voice.

'Get out of my pub, Bungie!' she yelled, when she had been restored to her senses. 'I never want you to darken my door again.' Thankfully, that particular job finished soon after and *Moonlight* moved on to other work, mainly the haulage of indivisible loads, for which her sturdy frame was ideal.

Meanwhile, the threshing business had grown, and the area covered was now considerable. Will Hearn, alias Shoot, and Will Chalk spent most of the threshing season in and around Hayes, Southall and Hanwell. George Ruff and I threshed corn around Rickmansworth, Denham, Chalfont and Chenies. Other sets were centred on Bovingdon, Watford, Amersham and Great Missenden.

We didn't have the market all to ourselves, however. There was competition from Sid Lofty in Amersham, Sonny Morton in Chesham and Mrs Abbot and

Jimmy Orchard in Hemel Hempstead. Beyond Great Missenden our gang would run up against Walter Stevens from Wendover, where he held sway. He had eight sets of tackle, mostly old Avelings and Fowlers plus a Wallis & Steevens compound. Clears of Burnham reached as far as the A4, the road which bisected both Slough and Reading.

It was pleasant work moving from farm to farm, and I liked being part of a team, but for Mr Tom it was tough business. He had to put up with the clamouring of farmers always demanding instant service and, what's more, each wanted their favourite driver to attend to their threshing. It was tough trying to keep everyone satisfied and the competition was fierce and, boy, getting paid was hard going.

As Christmas 1920 was drawing near Mr Tom had had enough, so he decided to sell up his threshing business. I couldn't believe it. Was I going to have to leave the family I had grown to love? George Ruff, with a moist eye, confirmed to me that Browns the Auctioneers from Tring had been instructed to sell all twelve sets by auction on 21 January 1921. Unsurprisingly, we could not find it in our hearts to celebrate Christmas that year.

Our last day's work was scheduled to be 14 January and when we had finished, we all trudged back to Amersham Common to be lined up along the bottom road to Chalfont & Latimer station (previously Chalfont Road). Next to Bell Lane stood

A Savage tractor. Mr Tom is seen far left.

A Fowell engine threshing near St Ives.

Black Jack's sister, *Gentle Edna*.

the Fowler ploughing tackle, then me and the other eleven sets of threshing tackle followed by some odd threshers and a trusser or two, where the auction started. It was the lowest day of my life thus far. To stand there and watch my fellow sets being sold was unbearable and the breakup of our gang marked the end of an era. By the time the auctioneer came round to me and my dear threshing machine partner, only one set had not been sold. Poor old *Croydon*, the high-wheeled Marshall, obviously hadn't appealed to anyone, and he looked very forlorn.

I lowered my oil lamps as the inevitable began. But, my dear master Mr Tom could not bear to see me sold, and so he bought me and my machine in. I was delighted but also sad to see my dear old friends depart. I cheered up a little when I discovered that the ploughing engines did not reach their reserve price, so they remained with us along with a few other odds and ends. It had been a cold, miserable and showery day and on the next it rained continuously. Getting us engines into line had made considerable ruts in the ground. Getting us out turned the meadow into a quagmire. The ground had to be levelled up and the scars from that sale took a long time to heal.

But steam goes on, and *Croydon* and I returned to our threshing. George Ruff was still my driver and Ding Burgin drove *Croydon*. But, of course, the problems associated with the threshing business hadn't gone away and getting paid was the

All lined up for sale, similar to the event at Bell Lane.

most prickly of them all. Farmers had always been slow payers; their business was, by definition, a slow process. In September they sowed the seed corn, they tended to it all through winter, reaped the crop in July and August, and then stacked it in ricks and left it there, often for months, before it was threshed into marketable grain. It could be sold to the miller six months later, potentially a whole two years after the original crop was sown. Only then, once farmers had the cash, would they then perhaps remember to pay for the threshing done all those months before.

Always the innovator, Mr Tom, came up with an idea to reduce significantly the amount of credit he had to provide. His proposal was to discount the price of the threshing by 2*s* 6*d*, if the farmer paid the driver and mate 1*s* 6*d* and 1*s* respectively, at the time of the threshing. Correspondingly, Mr Tom reduced the wages he paid the men by the same amount. This helped Mr Tom's cash flow considerably, and the idea was readily accepted by the farmers in our pleasant corner of the country. So well accepted was it, in fact, that the practice continued right up to the time when combine harvesters took over, which forever changed the way of life I had been used to for so long.

A Ruston Proctor busy on the threshing belt.

6

Peace in Our Time?

After the big auction sale threshing was now more of a side business, but I carried on as usual. We said goodbye, however, to *Croydon* and, in his stead, his driver Ding Burgin was now in charge of a Ransomes, Sims and Jefferies engine, No. 13696. Ding's round centred on Bovingdon and district. Their area was practically unaffected by the changes that were taking place in my territory. I had to cover a bigger area, as many an acre that had been used to produce wheat during the First World War was now laid down to grass. Not only that, but whole farms were rapidly disappearing under houses.

I remember Mr Tom once telling us that unlike other railway companies the Metropolitan was permitted to keep the excess land that hadn't been used when it built its lines out of London via Harrow to what were then rural communities like Uxbridge and Amersham. This enabled them to build houses on that land and then sell the dream of owning a home in the country close to a fast link to the centre of London. 'Metroland' was born, and it swallowed up large areas of my previous threshing rounds, creating whole new towns like Rayners Lane as a result.

My round extended as far as Ealing as well as Southall and Hayes and although I had to travel further between farms, I always had a full season's work throughout the 1920s and 1930s. During that period, I continued to make my annual visit to thresh corn at Hanwell Mental Hospital Farm. This job involved a rather hazardous journey, for in those days the electric trams terminated at Uxbridge. As I may have mentioned before, metal wheels on a combination of steel rails and granite setts were a villainous combination, and George always made sure we were well stocked with old sacks just in case.

Venturing deeper into those urban areas made accessing water for my boiler a sticky problem too. We could pick up from the popular watering hole where the River Pin passed under the A40 at the bottom of Hillingdon Hill on the road out of Uxbridge, but it was not unusual to arrive there thirsty only to discover a queue of engines waiting for their turn at the bridge. The deeply grooved coping stones on the parapet walls were, especially at the joints, evidence that over the years hundreds of wire armoured hose pipes had been slung over them by generations of steam transport drivers.

Here the steam waggons (the equivalent of today's heavy goods vehicles) that plied their trade between London and South Wales would replenish their tanks, in addition to the local haulage people and timber hauling engines. In that queue we would often espy the brewer Fuller Smith & Turner's Foden steam drays patiently waiting, along with engines from R. White's Lemonade. George Ruff once told me about the time when one of Fullers' drays collided with one of R. White's and the whole road was flooded with shandy! I'm not sure I believed him. But how I envied those Foden, Garrett and Sentinel steam waggons as they sped past me on their rubber tyres, while I plodded along the road on my steel wheels towards the Hanwell Iron Bridge towing my threshing machine, living van, chaff cutter and trusser!

While I was busy threshing, Mr Tom invested in more road rollers; he also acquired his first Foden steam waggon, soon to be followed by another. Road travel

A Boughton-owned Foden steam waggon.

Winters were colder and snowier.

A unique road roller converted from a Reading Ironworks traction engine.

was growing and growing. Cars were selling fast, and traffic was increasing so new highways had to be built to accommodate them, not to mention all the roads to the new houses that were being constructed. So, our road rollers were kept very busy whilst the steam waggons had plenty to occupy them as well. Consequently, the decision to diversify away from threshing allowed the firm to prosper throughout the 1920s.

However, things were about to change again. As the 1920s drew to a close, the next decade brought with it the Great Depression. In 1929, a crash on the stock market over 3,000 miles away had a massive impact around the world and the economy at home seemed to collapse. While I stayed busy, my steamroller friends had less and less to do; one by one they returned to Amersham when their contracts came to an end. At the lowest point of the Depression only two rollers were at work. During the winter of 1934 over twenty drivers had to be made redundant, and one dark evening George Ruff confided in me that he thought his turn might come next which worried me greatly, but fortunately we found enough things to do to keep us employed.

The Road Traffic Act 1934 only exacerbated the challenges which faced the road haulage industry. Draconian speed limits and heavy taxes (which corresponded

Fowler roller *Margaret* with Cyril Ruff at the wheel.

Ploughing engines earning their keep.

to axle weights) were applied to steam-powered vehicles and these measures, in effect, brought an end to steam lorries on the roads. Steam waggons were simply too heavy for the 'modern age'. Those wonderful Fodens, Sentinels and Garretts that used to rule the roads all headed to the scrapyard. All this new legislation added to the general decline, so much so, that there was no longer any congestion at the Pin Bridge. The change to diesel power cost millions of pounds at a time when there was very little money around. It had to come – the change was inevitable.

In addition to the transition to diesel on the road, the electricity revolution was taking place at home and a 'national grid' of transmission wires was being constructed so that every town and village could have access to this novel source of energy. In the Thames Valley where massive foundations for the electricity pylons were being dug, there was a great deal of pumping to undertake to keep the footings relatively dry. Several big engines, *Moonlight* amongst them, provided the steam muscle to power the 8- and 10-in centrifugal pumps specified, and *Rose*, an old 15-ton convertible road roller, donned her traction engine wheels to get stuck in too. The majority of this work was focussed on Staines and Laleham where the water table was particularly high. It was like hard labour, and it went on night and day for months.

As the decade progressed, much of the newspaper coverage was concerned about Herr Hitler and how he was drawing up expansionist plans in Germany. There couldn't be another war, could there? Almost unnoticed our government began making provisions just in case hostilities were to materialise. As a result, various things started to happen. I was dispatched to Benson in Oxfordshire to pull down trees and clear land to enlarge the aerodrome there and to construct a new road alignment around it. Other engine friends of mine were sent off to places much further away to carry out similar tasks. All over the country where the land was flat, preparation work for new airfields was being undertaken, and we were all kept extremely busy. But it was tough to witness whole farms disappear under concrete and all this upheaval added to the sense of uncertainty we felt about the future.

Despite the return of Mr Chamberlain from Munich in September 1938, waving that infamous piece of paper, the land clearing for new aerodromes gathered momentum. It was not long before my roller friends were back at work preparing new, massive runways for our aircraft. Meanwhile, I continued with my threshing, after all, we still needed to feed all these busy people. It was reassuring that despite all the changes that happened around me, we could still depend on the steady rhythm of the threshing season. However, as the distances I had to travel between farms kept expanding, to speed things up a bit, Mr Tom bought me a lovely present. He presented George and I with a set of rubber tyres. What a difference these made. I could now go much faster as my wheels were larger in diameter, and I no longer had to suffer the vibrations produced by my metal strakes.

Despite the continuing demand for threshing, in early 1939, Mr Tom announced that after nearly forty-four years, I was about to be retired. Deep down I knew this decision was coming as many of my moving parts were heavily worn and my firebox and boiler were long overdue for repairs. So, it looked like the upcoming threshing season was to be my last. However, in early September a crackly radio announcement by Mr Chamberlain declared that we were at war for the third time in my life. The government emphasised that it was all hands to the pump and that we should all be expected to 'make do and mend'. Consequently, I was granted a reprieve and promised an extensive overhaul. I received two brand-new gears, and Albert Locke, our excellent blacksmith, repaired my firebox so that it was as good as new. I was also fitted with a new set of boiler tubes and by the middle of October I was ready for work again, feeling as fit as a fiddle. But this time I was teamed up with a new driver, one Herbert Locke, Albert's younger brother, who had previously driven a road roller for the firm. He could drive an engine all right but had to learn the threshing business quickly, as did many others; and instead of a gang of men, we now had an army of land girls to help us with the threshers.

My old driver and friend George Ruff was instead put in charge of the maintenance of all the threshing machines, a job he appreciated as he no longer had to stay in a living van if we were working beyond cycling distance from his home. As time went on and more ground was put to the plough, it was apparent that more threshing machinery would be required; the pressure was on. George readily accepted the challenge that the job presented.

Mr Tom also repaired his old steam ploughing engines, and they were soon set to work reclaiming wet land on the Buckinghamshire/Bedfordshire border that had more or less lain dormant for twenty years. First, we had to clear the land of the bushes and trees, and when this was completed the ploughing engines were then employed to mole drain the waterlogged ground. Once the draining was finished, they would then plough the land. It was quite amazing to witness this transformation and just how little time it took to make the land productive again.

The firm was asked to take over operations in a large area of Hertfordshire where existing contractors were unable to expand. Mr Tom was soon in the market for more engines and threshing sets to meet this demand and his old friend, Lawrence Faulkner, at Leighton Buzzard possessed some spare. These were put into service as a temporary measure pending the delivery of several new machines from the Ministry of Agriculture.

All hands to the threshing for the war effort.

A Clayton and Shuttleworth towing a locomotive to be used for construction. The driver is Ding Burgin.

As more and more land was ploughed up our numbers grew dramatically and, before long, we had thirty-six sets of tackle at work, of which about twenty-five were steam-driven with the remainder powered by diesel tractors. As it was vital work providing as much food as possible to meet the demands of the war effort, there was a great deal of pressure put upon us and work was non-stop. We were now covering a huge area, and it required an enormous amount of managing, and a great deal of stores had to be provided to keep things running sweetly. It was a constant headache. Herbert Locke and I kept going until the end of 1945, when the war finally ended, and sadly we parted company when he returned to run his shop that his wife had looked after during the hostilities. However, I continued with several other drivers but two years later, in 1947, the curtain finally came down on my threshing career when I was retired for good. I couldn't credit it, but it had been fifty years since I first threshed corn and this time this really was the end.

Threshing with diesel tractors continued for a time but little by little the combine harvester took over. Our firm purchased a couple of Massey-Harris combines which they operated for a while, but it was not long before every cereal farmer had bought his own machine and so they didn't need Mr Tom's equipment anymore.

A pleasant pastoral scene from days gone by.

Sadly, things would never be the same again, and the sweet scent of steam intermingling with the smells of the farm was truly now a thing of the past. This time there was to be no reprieve. We engines had finally lost our own war, the battle against internal combustion. I suppose we knew that the end was coming, which is why we worked as hard as we did to prove our worth. But in the end, it was to no avail, the obnoxious odour of burnt hydrocarbons had taken over for good.

7

Retirement

When the day had come to hang up my threshing belt for the last time, I joined more than twenty or so of my old mates, consisting of steam ploughing engines, old steam tractors and road rollers along with rows of threshers and other obsolete equipment in the field at the back of the Bell Lane works. All these engines had been pressed back into service during the war and were now redundant. Amongst them were rollers Burrell No. 2037 and little McLaren No. 751, who had both spent their entire war in Scapa Flow, busily doing their bit for the War Office. Many of my friends I had worked with for years were there in the field, certainly tired, often completely worn out from the years of uninterrupted toil they had been called upon to undertake, but still proud products of an earlier, more sedate and gentler age where things were not so manic. It was very upsetting to see many of these wonderful steam engines sold for scrap to among others J. W. Hardwicks of West Ewell.

Black Jack begins his retirement.

Under wraps, wondering about the future.

An old Fowler surplus to requirements, awaiting her fate.

The threshers never even made it to the scrapyard, they simply rotted away, fading into the past, like the memories. In the end only two of us engines were left. Next to me stood the last traction engine ever to be built at my birthplace, the famous John Fowler and Sons Limited Steam Plough Works at Leeds. We stood and wondered what would become of us; my youngest brother engine was in fine shape and at thirty years my junior had never been off the farm where he worked all his life.

Day after day we awaited our fate in that field until one morning in 1948, some men turned up and set about cleaning and polishing me up. I was very keen to find out why. It turned out that a local ploughing match was to take place at Wendover Dean, and it was to be quite the occasion. There were to be trade stands and items of general interest too and the organisers thought it would be a good idea to add some equipment of an earlier age: horse-drawn ploughs and other implements including a threshing set at work.

So, off I went. It was a joyous afternoon. I was not only reunited with my old thresher and trusser but also with dear George Ruff, who along with Albert Philby took me to Wendover. We managed to recreate a reasonably authentic scene of fifty years earlier apart from my (well-worn) rubber tyres. We threshed wheat for about four hours in all. Some kind soul placed a small barrel of beer adjacent to my

Black Jack with his dear friend George Ruff (right) in 1948.

rear wheel and George, Albert and the gang of helpers together with some of the visitors made short work of the hoppy ale. It was a lovely day with lots of visitors, and everybody seemed to enjoy themselves to the full. Especially me. Despite the day being considered a resounding success, after this brief respite it was back to the familiar and melancholic surroundings of the field at Bell Lane, which had become a graveyard for out-of-date tackle.

I had heard, either from George or Albert, I am not sure whom, that I would not be scrapped, but instead preserved as a non-working showpiece at the entrance of the Boughton works. I suppose it made sense because my boiler was not in very good order and I badly needed repairs if ever I was to steam again, but nevertheless to not be able to feel the warmth of a fire inside me or steam moving through my cylinder would be things I knew I would miss very much.

But hope came at last. There had taken place a traction engine race between two gentlemen called Esmond Kimbell and Arthur Napper at a place called Appleford. The event caught the people's imagination and, soon after, rallies began to take place at various locations all over the country. As a result, it was decided that not only was I to be preserved as a showpiece, but that I would be admitted to the famous Walter Gower Hospital for steam engines at Bedford to have an operation to make me fit and well again too.

I was winched up on to a low-loader and off I went to Bedford. I was admitted for several weeks. Firstly, I was fitted with a new firebox and tube plate, and when

A Boughton team photo in the 1950s. Mr Tom is seen centre left.

they inspected my boiler barrel the doctors found it was so badly pitted in places that they made the decision to fit me with a new one. I also required a new back plate and part of my throat plate needed replacing; but at least my horn plates were all right. After all this had been attended to, I was reassembled and sent back to Amersham. But the work did not stop there. Once at home, all my moving parts were repaired or renewed. My worn-out gears were rebuilt by electric welding and, once more, my transmission was as good as new. I was even fitted with new rubber tyres. Finally, the big day arrived, and I was steamed up, all my new parts were tested and I became mobile once more. It was a wonderful feeling, one which at times I never thought I would experience again, and one or two close observers probably noticed a few tears in my oil lamps. But they were tears of joy.

Now that I was back to full health, I was able to go to all sorts of places and venues that I would never been able to visit during my working life. I visited dozens of rallies up and down the country, including the Great Dorset Steam Fair.

My proudest moment came when, in 1978, I was honoured with the role of hauling a Rolls-Royce RB211 jet engine mounted on a trailer in the Lord Mayor's Show in London. The Rolls-Royce of traction engines with the Rolls-Royce of aircraft engines! 1978 was the centennial year of the British Engine and Boiler Insurance Company which had always insured my boiler and as it also provided cover for the RB211 engine this is why I came to be chosen for this special task.

In preparation for the big day, I travelled up to London on Friday on a low-loader. I was woken up early on Saturday morning to get ready. A fire was lit and while

Black Jack showing off his threshing skills at a rally.

Right: Admirers learning about *Black Jack*'s history.

Below: *Black Jack* heading off to rally in the 1970s. John Bush is at the controls.

Black Jack towing the RB211 engine.

steam was rising, I was given an extra polish and bedecked with flags. Before I was fully ready my tender was filled with coal and water and, finally, I was coupled up to the trailer carrying the multi-million-pound engine.

My driver for the day was a director of our firm, Bernard Ruff, who was my dear old friend George's eldest son, so I felt in safe hands. He was accompanied by Tom Cavanagh, another good friend and sure hand at the wheel. While we waited in a side street with a whole lot of floats of every description until it was our time to move, my mind drifted back to the parade in Reading in 1897, all those years ago. It was funny that if you jumbled those numbers up you got 1978, and while I sat patiently awaiting my cue, that occasion all those years ago seemed like yesterday.

Finally, we received the signal to go. We were instructed to keep pace with the marching soldiers and bands. Just like last time, I managed that very well, as we travelled at a comfortable speed for me in low gear. I had no problem at all in pulling the load, but I did wonder how we would get on rolling down Ludgate Hill, after all, as you can well imagine, the modern trailer's brakes were not compatible with mine. I needn't have worried however, Bernard knew what he was doing and all went well, but I couldn't help letting out a sigh of steam of relief when the parade was over.

Of course, it was a great day out for thousands of people, who had made the effort to line the streets as we rumbled past. I know George Ruff and my dear old boss Mr Tom would have been proud to have seen us; we were all on television and watched by thousands of people as I pulled my very valuable load through the City of London.

There is an old proverb that goes 'After the Lord Mayor's Show came the shit cart'. Forgive my language please, but the great day was over. In what felt like a bit of an anticlimax I was soon back on the low-loader truck and conveyed back to Amersham to await my next assignment. Once back, I settled into my familiar routine. I hibernated all winter long at Honour's Yard, Lodge Lane, in Little Chalfont, just down the road from the Bell Lane works. Covered with heavy sheets and with a warm winter cap on my chimney, I would do my best to keep out the cold and try to snooze until the time when the days grew longer and warmer and the first fresh greens of springtime arrived. This would be the trigger for my keepers to uncover me and give me a wash and brush up, in preparation for the boiler inspector's annual visit who would give me a good going over.

A lot of people who undertake an annual medical, as it were, often suffer from nerves leading up to the big day. However, I never felt the jitters as I always knew I could rely on the engineering backup from my friends at Bell Lane, who had the resources and knowledge to sort out any issues and so it was that most times I would receive the OK.

However, on the odd occasion, elements of my boiler would have to be attended to. Sometimes I would have a new tube fitted, or get a broken stay fixed here and there. But with the repairs done, and with a freshly minted boiler certificate, I was ready for the road again and off we would go to places near and far to attend steam rallies and vintage fairs.

I loved these occasions, and who wouldn't? I would sit there, comfortably warm, ticking over, while receiving many admiring glances and comments. This happy

Taking part in a best engine in show competition.

Above: Being prepared for display by Henry Stevens, Barry's father.

Left: *Black Jack* reposing under his blankets one morning at a rally, *c*. 1983.

routine would continue throughout the summer until the season drew to a close as the nights grew longer. In most years, to round off the year there would be an end-of-season run-out to the Red Lion pub in my old home village of Chenies in the company of several other engines for a few pints and a good old chat about days long past.

One occasion stands out in the 1980s which brought back many memories. Bernard Ruff received a call from the council at Chorleywood House, a couple of miles down the road from the yard. A huge tree had had to be felled and needed to be recovered. Of course, Bernard had cut his teeth hauling similar types of timber and knew exactly what was needed to execute the undertaking successfully. I was woken up from a mid-summer slumber and a fire soon brought steam flowing through my veins and once ready, I was hitched up to an old pole waggon, another relic of times past, and we set off down the road.

On arrival, Bernard took in the full scale of the required operation. The tree's huge trunk was both long and with a marked dogleg in the middle. Unless it could be set accurately on the trailer, it might easily roll off and cause untold damage. With all the necessary equipment in place, Bernard instructed my crew for the day – Phil Honour and Roy Latchford – to reverse the trailer up alongside the log. They stopped when he thought he was in the right position. Bernard surveyed the scene and, as he did so, he took a long draw on one of his 'low fat' cigarettes, and turned to Phil, saying, 'Another two feet, if you please.'

I could tell Phil wasn't so sure, as I sensed a certain hesitancy at my controls, but nonetheless, he did as instructed. I inched the trailer back the necessary amount and, using my winch, rolled the trunk perfectly into position. What a triumph of skill and experience. Before long we headed off to the sawmill and thence back to the yard for a well-earned rest. A great day's work done, and one that evoked many happy memories, of olden skills and golden days.

Phil Honour and Tom Cavanagh pose with *Black Jack* outside Trafford's house.

Above: Bernard Ruff directing proceedings at Chorleywood House.

Left: *Black Jack* getting in position.

And so, the seasonal clock continued to tick around, the same timepiece as all those years ago but now set to a different way of life. Instead of working through the winter as I did in my younger days, braving the wind, rain and, more often than now, snow and ice, by the time November came round, the winter covers would be unfolded, and I would be wrapped up and tucked in until the sun's warmth returned.

8

1997: A Momentous Year

Nineteen years had passed since I was paired up with the Rolls-Royce engine during the Lord Mayor's Show and yet the time had passed in a flash. When my friends came to unwrap me in the spring, the first thing they did was wish me a very happy birthday. I was 100 years old. I certainly didn't feel that aged, and as I was once again being prepared for my boiler inspection, I certainly thought that my health was first class. The examiner agreed and signed the certificate permitting me to be insured to carry 140 lb of pressure, not bad for one who has just reached 100 years in one family's ownership.

Black Jack, Bernard, Phil Honour and Roy Latchford pose having successfully loaded the tree.

However, some of my drive gears were very worn, creating so much play that my flywheel would turn quite the amount before my wheels moved and the clatter of teeth produced a sound like an old telephone. So, the decision was taken for me to get some new gears cut and also for me to get a brand-new coat of paint.

By early June, I was freshly out of the Bell Lane workshops resplendent in my shining black, carefully lined out with amber and red and ready for the first engagement of my centenary year. Of course, it wasn't just me celebrating 100 years of existence, the Boughton family business established all those years ago by my dear friend and owner young Mr Tom was also preparing to mark the occasion.

Firstly, I was off to the sunny climes of South Devon where the Institute of Wastes Management was holding its annual conference and exhibition on Paignton seafront. Manufacturing equipment for the waste industry was one of the areas the Boughton firm excelled in. Manoeuvred into pride of place on the Boughton stand, I spent a week gently ticking over in the warm sunshine. My mind kept

Prepared for repairs in spring 1997.

drifting back to Prospect Park 100 years earlier when I first sat on a stand, ticking over gently trying to attract the attention of a prospective buyer. This time round, of course, I had no trouble attracting attention. Everyone walking past would stop to take in the sight of a 100-year-old traction engine simmering gently in front of the row of hotels and boarding houses along the esplanade. In front of me, was an information board with the picture of me heading up the diamond jubilee parade in 1897.

Once we were back in Buckinghamshire, a rerun of my original trip from Reading to Chenies on 14–15 July 1897 was planned to take place exactly 100 years later. I could not exactly follow the same route. A century ago, when I first undertook that journey, there were no such things as one-way streets or roundabouts, let alone town bypasses. However, overall, we stuck to the spirit of the venture as closely as possible. This time Mr Tom's grandson, Edward, drove much of the way, and thankfully the journey passed without incident, my hose pipe remained securely fastened, for example. However, instead of meeting shying horses, we just encountered a terrific amount of road traffic instead. What a difference 100 years had made.

We made a detour to the Bell Lane works in Amersham for a photo session with the Boughton family and then continued on to Chenies Manor to complete the

Posing at the IWM show in 1997 by the seaside.

Left: *Black Jack* arriving at Bell Lane having almost completed his re-enactment of his first journey 100 years before.

Below: Members of the Boughton family, with Trafford in the centre, pose with *Black Jack* on his 100th birthday.

Black Jack poses at the entrance to the Bell Lane works.

journey, fortunately without smashing any gates. On arrival, we were greeted by the then owner of the manor, and after having had my picture taken in what was the farmyard of my youth (what echoes there were of those times long past), it was back to Lodge Lane for a few days' rest before my next rallying call.

Later that year, in August, I was driven from Little Chalfont all the way to the Great Dorset Steam Fair, not a bad journey for a 100-year-old. 1997 was a special Fowler year at the show, and I took pride of place amongst my fellow engines. It was a very proud moment for me.

9

A New Century

The rhythm of the seasons continued. The winter rests followed by busy summers travelling up and down the country to rallies and gatherings far and wide kept me very busy and before I knew it, the year 2000 was upon us. Thus it was that I not only entered my second millennium but also my third century. This was a testament to the craft and skill of the workers at John Fowler and Son, but even they probably didn't envisage that I would still be steaming over 100 years later, and could George Chapman, the Fowler salesman, have imagined that the family he sold me to in 1897 were still my owners in the year 2000?

As the summer progressed, I started to not feel myself. I was suffering from pains in my boiler and although I did my best to communicate this to my driver, it was to no avail. One day late in the season we were preparing for a trip out to the Royal Standard pub, near Beaconsfield, to celebrate the fortieth anniversary of the first Chiltern rally, and as I headed out of Honour's Yard, I felt a sharp pain and steam started bleeding from my boiler into the firebox. Naturally, this confused my poor driver, and after he had brought me to a halt, he called for help.

Moments later it became obvious that I was in serious trouble and any thoughts of a nice day out evaporated as the last pounds of steam pressure seeped out of my boiler, leaving me feeling totally empty and strangely chilled. This was the first time I had suffered a serious breakdown in my 103-year-old life, and I was devastated.

To make matters worse, the Boughton business was no longer in family ownership and all the skilled men and tools capable of effecting repairs had long since been moved on by the new owners who attached scant value to such things. However, it soon transpired that what was wrong with me would take even more than their impressive abilities, and only a prolonged stay at a specialist traction engine hospital would enable me to recover. In short, I had suffered from what I learnt was known as a 'catastrophic failure'.

Above: The former entrance to the Bell Lane works in 2025.

Below: A reminder of the Boughton works in Little Chalfont.

Sadly, there were few companies that could undertake the level of repair estimated, and it was necessary to engage the expert services of A. G. Bicknell and Co. Ltd in Liphook, Hampshire, to take on the responsibility. My family's financial resources were also much more limited and the guesstimated bill to restore me to full health was going to be shockingly expensive, and a method of funding my repairs needed to be established or I would most likely end up a static display in a museum, or even worse.

Firstly, before I could even go to Bicknell's, it was necessary that I was dismantled in order to get to the heart of the problem. Enter stage right two of my best friends, Phil Honour and Barry Stevens, two kinder and more skilled men I couldn't name. They had generously volunteered to undertake the huge task of preparing me for the operation, by carefully taking me apart. I was nervous but knew I was in the safest hands possible. Of course, Phil and Barry could only work on me when they had the spare time, and for me it resulted in a long wait.

Therefore, for what seemed a lifetime, I sat in the yard under my tarpaulins cold and lonely, waiting for when the lads got the opportunity to get started. It was hard not to let melancholic thoughts occupy my mind. Would I ever feel the warm and life-affirming sensation of steam in my cylinder again? Every time someone lifted the corner of my tarpaulin to check me over, my hopes shot up, but they would soon replace the covers and leave me to my musings. I lost track of the passage of time, and the seasons all seemed to blur into one without the familiar routine and its timely punctuation marks. Somehow, though, I knew that there had to be a valid explanation as to why I had been left for so long. So, I resigned myself to adopting the philosophical view that had served me so well throughout my long working career and contented myself with recalling all the many happy memories I had stored from the past.

I was just settling into an early spring's threshing session, with George at my controls and the sweet scent of warm oil and steam weaving its way through the farmer's skilfully constructed and fragrant hayricks, when I registered a couple of familiar voices and woke to the realisation that my covers weren't just being lifted but were being taken off entirely. Finally, after the long wait, things were beginning to happen.

'I can't believe it's been five years, Baz,' Phil Honour exclaimed as the two of them inspected the toll the years had taken on me. 'He looks blooming good on it, all considered.' It must be 2005, I thought, I could not believe it. Once they got underway, and the extent of my injuries was revealed, the more it became apparent that I would need a lot of work. The thorny issue of how to pay the bill came sharply back into focus.

As I mentioned, family resources were depleted, and just when it seemed impossible to accumulate the necessary finances, one of my old workmates came

Under wraps and out of service.

rolling to the rescue when I least expected it. It was my dear colleague *Alice*, a large Fowler road roller, who had provided many years of loyal service back in the day but since then had been sadly languishing in pieces for decades, an even further distance from feeling steam in her chest once again. She was in desperate need of a kind benefactor to restore her to full health, and it seemed a forlorn hope that such a suitable knight in shining armour could be found. But, and with almost perfect timing, negotiations suddenly got underway with just such an individual and not long after a deal was struck! It was with immense relief that before long, *Alice* was being carefully loaded onto a transport and heading off to her new home leaving behind the required finances to service my repair bill. Not for the first time in my life was victory grabbed from the jaws of defeat.

Once Phil and Barry had completed the careful dismantling required by Bicknell's, I had basically been reduced to a bare boiler and firebox assembly, virtually unrecognisable as a proud product of the John Fowler Steam Works. On arrival at Liphook, I was carefully examined, and a surgical plan was drafted of what needed doing and in what order. I was out for nearly a year and when I came round, it transpired that I had received a new firebox, a new tube and throat plate, and, most significantly, the bottom half of my boiler had had to be completely replaced. What's more, because the new firebox was of a rivetted construction, my previous one being welded, a fresh foundation ring was required as well. It was

Ready to head off for surgery.

hard to credit how long I had been under the surgeons' tools but as the staff at Bicknell's kept reminding me, this sort of craftmanship can't be rushed.

I was eager to return home and start to feel myself again, but before I could be discharged, I had to demonstrate that I could hold pressure, and a challenging hydraulic examination ensued. When I had successfully passed, I was finally allowed to be taken back to Honour's Yard. I can't emphasise too much how great a feeling that was.

Once home, so began the time-consuming task of piecing me back together. Barry soon encountered a problem with my horn plates (the sheets of metal mounted to the boiler which support the axle), and so before I knew it, I was returning to Bicknell's for a further operation.

Once back again at Honour's Yard, slowly but surely, I began to take shape, thanks to the enduring efforts of my friends Barry and Phil. Several times, they encountered issues they were not expecting and that necessitated patience-draining adjustments and much slog and toil, but painstakingly over weekend after weekend, I began to resemble a proud Fowler engine once more.

Right: Returning from Bicknell's.

Below: Preparing *Black Jack*'s front axle for the wheels.

Black Jack is starting to come together.

Left: *Black Jack* is reunited with his chimney.

Below: The boiler lagging is completed.

Such was the time taken to piece me back together that when I was (finally) ready to feel warmth inside again, the hydraulic certification that took place at Bicknell's had expired and I required a revalidation. It was difficult to credit that it had been so long since I had come round from the first operation, but we all felt that, at last, we were on the home straight.

Above: Almost finished.

Right: A fire is lit.

On the day of the check, naturally everyone was nervous, after all, it had been almost sixteen years since I had felt the comforting warmth of a fire and the pleasant sensation of steam pressure rising inside my boiler. However, we needn't have worried; I passed with flying colours and with the final touches soon completed I was restored to full health. We enjoyed a good celebration that day!

Left: Steam is building nicely.

Below: The safety valve works as it should.

Black Jack moves under his own steam for the first time in sixteen years.

10

To the Present Day

Naturally, as befits anyone who is over 119 years old, I would have to take things a bit easier and I realised that my summers weren't going to be as packed as they once were, but it was so good to feel tarmac under my wheels and the (albeit languid) slipstream around my funnel, that any trip out would be like a gift from the traction engine gods. My first public appearance was a visit to the pub in Little Chalfont, and it was an opportunity show off my new paintwork

Black Jack resting outside the pub on his first outing in years.

Black Jack on his way home.

which was now plain black; the lack of the amber and red lining gave me a more purposeful and business-like appearance which harked back to how I looked during my working life.

Also absent was my brass chimney top. This had been the casualty of an incident on my way back from the Great Dorset Steam Fair in 1997. I had been gently slumbering on the back of a low-loader, when the driver opted to pass under the Metropolitan Railway Line's bridge near Chalfont & Latimer station. Next a deafening clanging noise jarred me awake and I watched my funnel rolling across the road. He had forgotten the necessary height clearance required.

I eased myself gently into the new routine, a routine that befitted someone of my venerability. However, I had clearly not lost any of that famous Fowler pedigree. In July 2018, Phil and Barry took me to an aerodrome at South Cerney in Gloucestershire where a steam rally was in full swing. Holding centre stage was a large portable bench saw, of a similar type that I used to cut timber with between the threshing seasons. No engine was attached, however, so Phil headed over to the saw's owner to enquire if he would like me to drive it for a while.

'What that old engine?' the sawbones replied with an arched, incredulous gaze. 'Do you really think it (!) could keep up with my saw?'

I looked at Phil and clocked the calm and placid demeanour that came over his face, which always preceded a knowing and emphatic retort. 'What you actually mean is, can your saw keep up with this engine!' A few moments later and with my flywheel belted up to his device, sawbones willingly conceded he was wrong. I still had it.

I have been privileged to have two such wonderful pals. They often remind me of my dear departed friend George Ruff, with whom I enjoyed such a lengthy and happy partnership, and it is the close nature of our present relationship which only pains me more when I recall an unfortunate incident that happened about three years ago. We had been at a rally over at Quainton in Buckinghamshire and I was

Black Jack basking in the sun at a rally in 2019.

on the low-loader ready to return home. Phil and Barry always removed my funnel to avoid any repeat of my railway bridge experience. As Phil started to lower it, a devilish combination of oily hands and greasy metal resulted in it slipping through his fingers, but in an heroic attempt to save it from falling, it ended up slamming into poor Phil's shoulder with a bone-breaking crunch. It had fractured his collar bone, and he was out of action for six weeks. I felt so sorry for him.

In 2023, I was woken in April, which seemed early for the summer season and soon a warming fire was crackling in my firebox and beginning to heat the fresh water in my boiler. I learnt that we were making the short trip to my first home, Chenies Manor, just down the road. It transpired that the Road Locomotive Society (RLS) wished to recreate a scene that had been captured on camera exactly 100 years before. It had occurred to the periodical's producers that both the engine and the scene had not changed much in the intervening century and that it would be a great opportunity to capture a modern-day version of that picture. I was manoeuvred into position in the manor's farmyard, as close to the original as possible. The photos captured a remarkable full-circle story.

As we approach the present day, in addition to the rally commitments I undertake in the summer months, my family owners attempt to organise a gathering once a year so that we can all get together to swap stories, old and new, and just relax

Black Jack at Chenies Manor in 1923.

Black Jack at Chenies Manor in 2023.

in the heady perfume of steam and warm oil for a short while, a welcome break from the modern-day astringent smells and strident noises. It is an occasion I look forward to immensely, as it reminds me of the times when I was a valued member of a big team taking on the challenges of a busy working life. Of course, in one way I could cut a lonely figure, what with so many of my human and engine companions now mere ghosts, but instead, I delight in the friends and family that I still have and the history we share.

It does not fall to me to say that my life story has been remarkable. I am, after all, a humble general-purpose Fowler traction engine, one of a batch that just happened to be sold to a particular individual in Buckinghamshire. But it is a story that has one consistent theme running through it that is quite special, and that is a 129-year (and counting) association with one family. We have been through thick and thin together. I like to think I contributed in no small way to the prosperity the Boughton family business enjoyed over the years, and that I can still help now, by providing a connection down the ages that links dear young Mr Tom with the Boughton family members who still own me today. Let's not forget, too, that both Phil and Barry also have family connections associated with the Boughton business that span the generations and between us all we share a common history and, hopefully, future too. As I approach my 130th year, I look back with pride, but more importantly, I look forward with hope. I feel valued and loved and with that support, who knows, how many years we can keep steaming along together.

Black Jack at the Amersham Heritage Day, September 2025.

Postscript

It has been an absolute pleasure to work on this book. My father's memory and attention to historical detail were remarkable and it was a joy to read such an in-depth account of life from more than 100 years ago. This connection with the past is so valuable, particularly when it comes to everyday history, as this is so rarely recorded for posterity. The joy of unearthing the little details is probably the most satisfying. Specifics such as the worn stones at the river crossing in Uxbridge where the engines lowered their suction hoses to lift water up into their tenders bring the story to vibrant life; I hope you agree.

Black Jack's story is truly remarkable and one which has few peers. For one engine to remain in the same family's ownership for such a long time is impressive enough, but the fact that that ownership commenced from new is all the rarer.

Astronomers say that looking into the night sky enables us to look far into the past, in fact millions of years. However, the problem with that notion is that it is hard for us to fully grasp the concept of such a long period of time. I would counter instead that seeing, and indeed touching, *Black Jack* achieves a better sense of time travel, as 129 years is an amount of time which is far easier to conceive. Indeed, it is all the more valuable as the past century has also been the most remarkable phase of human history, just witness the technological advances, the industrialisation and sadly the destruction too. Perhaps *Black Jack*'s appearance towing the jet engine at the 1978 Lord Mayor's Show most succinctly sums this up. In parenthesis, will an RB211 still be working in 2078, I wonder?

Black Jack is a time machine that we can all enjoy through this medium of such a rich collection of stories that I hope this small book goes some way to preserve for posterity.